PATRICK AND THE DUCKLING

By

Dorothy Haas

Illustrated by

Art Seiden

PRINTED IN GREAT BRITAIN
DEAN & SON Ltd.
52/54 Southwark St. LONDON SE1 1UA
TRADE MARK

This edition published by Dean & Son Ltd., 1979
0 603 00148 3

KEEP OFF

Once upon a time in a public park there was a policeman called Patrick. He stood in the sun all day, twirling his stick and saying, "How d'ye do?" and, "Sure 'n' it *is* a fine day!" to people.

Patrick looked after things.

And once upon a time, in that park, there was a duckling. He lived near the pond and ate corn and crumbs, and swam about, and dunked for fun. He didn't know Patrick and Patrick didn't know him.

Now one day the duckling looked up the path that led away from the pond.

"I wonder what's there," he said to himself, and, "I just guess I'll find out, I-guess-I-guess."

And so he followed the path.

Before long he saw chittery-chattery animals that swung by their tails.

He saw big brown animals that growled and begged for peanuts.

He saw large lazy animals that roared and switched their tails.

He saw animals with long necks.

He saw animals with long noses.

He saw shiny shoes. He saw — *shiny shoes?* The duckling looked up... and up... and up at —

Patrick.

"Well, now," chuckled Patrick. "Is it a duck we have here, tramping up and down our public paths disturbing the nice neat gravel?"

Patrick shared his popcorn with the duckling. And then he picked him up and carried him back to the pond.

"Ponds are for ducks and ducks are for ponds," he said, and went away up the path whistling.

But the duckling liked the things he had seen in the park. And so each day after that he followed the path and saw strange and wonderful things.

He saw the animals with long necks and the animals with long noses. He saw animals with long horns. He saw animals that

carried their babies with them. He saw striped animals and spotted animals. And he always saw Patrick. *That* was best of all. Patrick always shared his popcorn with him. But then Patrick always carried him back to the pond saying, "Ponds are for ducks and ducks are for ponds."

Now one day, at the pond, the duckling heard a great frightened quacking. He hurried to the other ducks and found them caught in a tangled string net some boys had dropped over them. The ducks quacked and fluttered their wings, but they could not get free.

"Wait," said the duckling. "Wait!" And he hurried up the path, past the chittery-chattery animals, the growling animals, the roaring animals, until he found Patrick.

"Quick!" he quacked. "Quick! Quick!"

"Quick, is it now?" said Patrick, and followed the duckling to the pond.

There he found the ducks in the string net and set them free. Then he gave a good talking-to to those boys. The boys hung their heads and promised to come back every day for a week to feed pop-corn and pieces of apple to the ducks.

At last he turned to the duckling.

"Now that was a good and brave deed for a duckling to do," he said, "and I'm thinking I need someone to help me on my rounds. Duckling, how would you be feeling about that?"

"Quack!" said the duckling flapping his wings *very* hard. "Quack! Quack!"

And so never again did Patrick carry the duckling back to the pond, saying, "Ponds are for ducks, and ducks are for ponds." Instead, together, Patrick and the duckling looked after things in the public park.